50 WAYS WITH

SALADS

50 WAYS WITH

SALADS

KATHARINE BLAKEMORE

LANSDOWNE

Published by Lansdowne Publishing Pty Ltd.
Level 5, 70 George Street, Sydney NSW 2000, Australia

Managing Director: Jane Curry
Production Manager: Sally Stokes

First published by Weldon Publishing in 1991
Reprinted in this expanded edition, with color plates 1993
Reprinted 1994

Designed by Kathie Baxter Smith
Photography by Andrew Elton
Food Styling by Mary Harris
Recipes typeset in Granjon by Character, North Sydney
Printed in Singapore by Tien Wah Press (Pte) Ltd

National Library of Australia Cataloguing-in-Publication data

Blakemore, Katharine.
50 ways with salads.

Rev. ed.
Includes index.
ISBN 1 86302 330 5.
1. Salads. I. Title. II. Title: Fifty ways with salads.

641.83

Front cover photograph: Steamed Vegetable Salad, recipe page 90
Page 2: Tuna and Pasta Salad, recipe page 98
Pages 8 & 9: Smoked Salmon and Avocado Salad, recipe page 80
Back cover photograph: Sweet and Sour Mushroom Salad, recipe page 92

CONTENTS

INTRODUCTION

A salad is a mixture of raw or cooked foods which are seasoned, and usually served with a dressing.

A salad is a most versatile dish. It can be served as a first course, accompany a principal dish or be a main course in its own right. Substantial meat or fish salads or an interesting mixture of these dishes can make a magnificent focal point to a meal.

The basic salad is made up of green leaf vegetables: just one lettuce, or a combination of the many varieties that are now readily available such as lollo rosso, batavia and lamb's lettuce. Raw spinach, Belgian endive (chicory) and watercress can also be added to a green salad. These salads are usually dressed with a vinaigrette dressing and served as an accompaniment to grilled or cold meat or an omelet. With the addition, however, of such ingredients as avocado, goat's cheese, crisply grilled bacon or croutons, a green salad becomes a delicious first course, light lunch or supper dish.

Made with the freshest and most nutritious ingredients, salads have many advantages, besides the vitamin — and protein — rich foods that go into them. They can contain entirely raw components, so no special skills are required from the cook and none of the goodness is taken from the food by heating. It is very important when buying food for salads, especially those made from raw vegetables and fruit, that only the freshest and best quality ingredients are used. It is uneconomical to buy, for example, cheap wilted lettuces, as most of the leaves will have to be discarded.

Most salads can be prepared in advance, which is very useful when entertaining, and others can be assembled in a matter of minutes. For salad making no specialized equipment is required apart from a chopping board, a sharp knife and a large mixing bowl, although a salad spinner for rinsing and drying green leaf vegetables is a handy aid.

Above all, salads can look and taste infinitely appetizing. They range from the simple glistening mixture of bright green lettuce leaves and red and yellow tomatoes in a glass bowl, to the most exotic combination of Asian vegetables, noodles and spices. It is worth giving some thought to the dishes used to serve the salads in order to show the food off to its best advantage. Make sure that the serving dish does not clash with the food being served in it. The brighter and more exotic combinations are best served on plain dishes. Take a little time too, in decoratively arranging the food, as it should be pleasing to the eye as well as the palate.

Salads have been thought of in the past as cold dishes, but a current trend is for them to be served warm, as you will see from examples in this book. Most other salads are best if served at room temperature, as a lot of character can be lost if food is served too cold.

Texture is an important characteristic, so even when salad vegetables are cooked they should remain crisp or firm. Nuts and seeds add different shapes and consistency to a salad mixture, besides being good sources of protein.

Herbs greatly enhance a salad, especially fresh ones. If only dried herbs are available, use sparingly as their taste impact can be quite intense. Likewise, take care with other seasonings, especially salt, which is often not necessary with strong elements such as blue cheese and smoked fish.

Dressings are considered essential to most salads and there is a wide variety of the traditional ingredients — oil and vinegar — to choose from. Extra virgin olive oil is the best quality olive oil but light sunflower or vegetable oils are popular, and good grapeseed, sesame and nut oils are available.

There are fine wine, fruit, sherry and herb vinegars on the market and many different mustards and peppers, so experiment with different combinations. Other dressings are based on mayonnaise or yogurt; wherever possible, use the low fat or light versions of these products.

It is not necessary to stick rigidly to each recipe. If an ingredient is not available, or not to your taste, substitute another and be inventive. Above all, whatever the combination, a salad should be a bright and nutritious dish.

THE RECIPES

BEEF SALAD NIÇOISE

3 tablespoons olive oil
1 onion, chopped
1 clove garlic, crushed
2 cups (8 oz, 250 g) eggplant
(aubergine), cubed
1 large green bell pepper
(capsicum), chopped
2 cups (8 oz, 250 g) zucchini
(courgettes), sliced
2 cups (1 lb, 500 g) tomatoes,
skinned, seeded and chopped
1 teaspoon dried basil
1 tablespoon red wine vinegar
salt and freshly ground black
pepper
8–12 slices rare roast beef
12 black olives

Heat oil in a large pan, add onion, garlic and eggplant. Cover pan and cook until soft.

Add bell pepper, zucchini, tomatoes and basil, cook uncovered for about 10 minutes, stirring occasionally.

Remove from the heat, let stand until cold, then stir in vinegar, salt and pepper.

Lay the slices of beef overlapping on an oval serving dish, spoon the cold vegetables around the edge.

Arrange the olives on top of the vegetables.

Preparation time 20 minutes plus standing time
Cooking time 20 minutes
Serves 4 to 6

Advance preparation: The vegetables can be cooked up to 1 day in advance. Keep covered in the refrigerator. Assemble the dish just before serving.

BEET AND ORANGE SALAD

1 oak leaf lettuce
4 oranges
12 oz (375 g) cooked beets
   (beetroot)
1 tablespoon orange juice
3 tablespoons sunflower oil
2 teaspoons clear honey
1 teaspoon whole-grain mustard
salt and freshly ground black
   pepper

Line an oval serving platter with the lettuce.

Remove the zest from the oranges with a zester and reserve.

Remove any remaining rind and pith from the oranges, then cut them into slices. Arrange on top of the lettuce.

Slice the beets and arrange them over the oranges.

Mix together the orange juice, oil, honey, mustard, salt and pepper. Pour over the salad then sprinkle with the reserved orange zest.

Preparation time 15 minutes
Serves 4

BITTERSWEET SALAD

*2 large heads Belgian endive
(chicory)*
*1 red-skinned apple, cored and
cubed*
*1 large orange, peeled and
segmented*
*1 cup (4 oz, 125 g) black grapes,
halved and pipped*
*1 cup (4 oz, 125 g) mixed pecan,
brazil and hazelnuts, roughly
chopped*
1 tablespoon orange juice
*3 tablespoons thick unflavored
(natural) yogurt*
*1 tablespoon walnut or hazelnut
oil*
2 teaspoons clear honey
*salt and freshly ground black
pepper*

Trim the bases and remove the core from the Belgian endive. Reserve 8 large outside leaves, thinly slice the remainder.

Put sliced endive into a bowl, add the apple, orange, grapes and nuts.

Mix together orange juice, yogurt, oil, honey, salt and pepper. Add to the fruit and nuts.

Put reserved Belgian endive leaves in a circle around a serving dish. Divide the mixture among the leaves. Put any remaining mixture into the center of the dish.

Preparation time 15 minutes
Serves 4

CARROT, NUT AND RAISIN SALAD

1 lb (500 g) carrots, peeled
1 small green bell pepper
  (capsicum), chopped
½ cup (2 oz, 50 g) dry roast
  peanuts
½ cup (3 oz, 75 g) seedless raisins
1 tablespoon poppy seeds
grated rind and juice of 1 orange
2 tablespoons sunflower oil
1 teaspoon French mustard

Coarsely grate carrots into a bowl, add bell pepper, peanuts, raisins and poppy seeds.

Beat together orange rind and juice, oil and mustard. Pour dressing over carrots and mix well.

Preparation time 15 minutes
Serves 4

Advance preparation: If preparing this salad in advance do not add the nuts until just before serving to keep them crisp.

CHICKEN, MELON AND MANGO SALAD

4 × 4 oz (125 g) cooked, boned
   chicken breasts
1 small yellow-fleshed melon
2 mangoes, peeled
2 tablespoons mango chutney
3 tablespoons sunflower oil
1 tablespoon lemon juice
½ teaspoon mild curry powder
1 teaspoon grated fresh ginger
1 small lettuce
1 tablespoon toasted sesame seeds

Cut the chicken into small pieces, put it into a bowl.

Discard seeds from the melon, make into balls or cut into small cubes. Cut mango into cubes. Add melon and mango to the chicken.

Finely chop any large pieces of mango from the chutney. Mix with the oil, lemon juice, curry powder and ginger. Add to the bowl; stir gently to coat with dressing.

Line a serving plate with the lettuce leaves. Pile the chicken and mango mixture into the center. Sprinkle with the sesame seeds.

Preparation time 20 minutes
Serves 4

Variation: A small pineapple could be used instead of the melon.

Note: This dish would make an ideal starter for 8 people.

CHINESE SALAD

3 oz (75 g) whole baby corn cobs
3 oz (75 g) mange-tout
   (snow-peas)
salt
3 cups (6 oz, 175 g) beansprouts
3 cups (6 oz, 175 g) Nappa
   cabbage (Chinese leaves),
   shredded
1 red bell pepper (capsicum),
   seeded and cut into strips
1 cup (6 oz, 175 g) peeled shrimp
   (prawns)
2 tablespoons sesame oil
2 tablespoons light soy sauce
½ teaspoon Chinese five spice
   powder
1 teaspoon grated fresh ginger
freshly ground black pepper

Cook the baby corn and mange-tout in lightly salted boiling water for 3 minutes. Drain then cool under running cold water. Dry on paper towels.

Put into a salad bowl with the beansprouts and Nappa cabbage, red bell pepper and shrimp.

Mix together the remaining ingredients, pour into the bowl and mix well.

Preparation time 20 minutes
Cooking time 3 minutes
Serves 6

Variation: This salad could also be made with 6 oz (175 g) thinly sliced roast pork instead of the shrimp.

CRAB AND ARTICHOKE SALAD

*2 cups (8 oz, 250 g) white crab
    meat — fresh, frozen or
    canned*
*6–7 canned artichoke bases,
    quartered*
½ cucumber, cubed
12 radishes, halved
2 tablespoons crème fraîche
1 tablespoon grapefruit juice
*salt and freshly ground black
    pepper*
bunch watercress
2 pink-fleshed grapefruit

Put the crab meat into a bowl, add the artichoke bases, cucumber and radishes.

Beat the crème fraîche until thick; add the grapefruit juice, salt and pepper. Add to the crab mixture, mix gently but thoroughly.

Arrange the watercress around the edge of a shallow dish. Put the crab salad into the center.

Peel and segment the grapefruit, removing all the white pith. Put the grapefruit segments in a circle on top of the crab salad.

Preparation time 20 minutes
Serves 4

Watchpoint: Always pick over crab meat, whether fresh, frozen or canned in case any small fragments of shell remain.

CRACKED WHEAT SALAD

1¾ cups (8 oz, 250 g) cracked
    wheat (bulghar)
1 bunch scallions (green onions,
    spring onions), finely chopped
1 bunch parsley, finely chopped
1 bunch mint, finely chopped
juice of 1 lemon
⅔ cup (¼ pint, 150 ml) olive oil
salt and freshly ground black
    pepper
½ small cucumber, sliced
8 oz (250 g) tomatoes, thinly sliced
1 onion, sliced
fresh mint sprigs

Put cracked wheat into a bowl, cover with cold water. Let stand for 30 minutes. Drain well, squeezing out as much water as possible.

Put back into the bowl; add scallions, parsley, mint, lemon juice, olive oil, salt and pepper and mix thoroughly.

Turn out into a serving dish. Arrange alternate slices of cucumber and tomato around the salad. Garnish with onion rings and mint sprigs.

Preparation time 20 minutes plus standing time
Serves 4 to 6

Advance preparation: This salad can be prepared up to 2 days in advance to allow the cracked wheat to absorb all the flavors. Keep covered and chilled. Do not add the cucumber, tomatoes and garnishes until just before serving.

CRISPY DUCK SALAD

4 × 6 oz (175 g) duck breasts
2 thick slices white bread, crusts
 removed and cubed
2 tablespoons vegetable oil
3 tablespoons cranberry sauce
½ teaspoon powdered ginger
1 tablespoon orange juice
1 tablespoon red wine vinegar
salt and pepper, to taste
6 oz (175 g) mixed lettuce leaves
8 kumquats, sliced

Broil (grill) the duck breasts, skin side down for about 10 minutes. Turn skin side up and broil for a further 10 minutes until skin is crisp and duck is cooked through. Let stand until cool.

Fry the bread cubes in hot oil until crisp and browned. Drain well on paper towels.

Mix together the cranberry sauce, ginger, orange juice and vinegar. Taste and adjust seasoning.

Toss the lettuce leaves in the cranberry dressing, divide among 4 plates, putting them to one side of the plate. Sprinkle with the fried bread cubes.

Slice the duck breasts diagonally. Fan out down the side of the plates. Lay the kumquat slices along the duck.

Preparation time 15 minutes
Cooking time 20 minutes
Serves 4

Note: Most supermarkets now sell packets of ready prepared mixed salad leaves but if these are unavailable use an escarole (curly endive) instead.

CRUNCHY LEEK SALAD

1 lb (500 g) young leeks, sliced
salt
2 tablespoons sesame oil
1 tablespoon sunflower oil
1 tablespoon lemon juice
1 tablespoon sunflower seeds
1 tablespoon pumpkin seeds
1 tablespoon sesame seeds
12 thin slices prosciutto
   (Parma ham)

Cook the leeks in lightly salted boiling water for 3 to 5 minutes until just tender. Drain well, put into a bowl; add the sesame and sunflower oils and lemon juice. Mix well then let stand until cold.

Mix the seeds together, spread onto a baking sheet, and cook in the oven 425°F (220°C, Gas Mark 7) for about 5 minutes until lightly browned. Remove from the oven, let stand until cold.

Divide prosciutto among 4 plates. Put an equal amount of leeks on top of the ham. Sprinkle the leeks with the toasted seeds.

Preparation time 10 minutes
Cooking time 10 minutes
Serves 4

EGGPLANT (AUBERGINE) AND TAHINI SALAD

1½ lb (750 g) eggplants
  (aubergines)
salt
3 tablespoons olive oil
1 clove garlic, crushed
½ cup (2 oz, 50 g) black olives
1 tablespoon wine vinegar
2 tablespoons tahini (sesame paste)
2 tablespoons unflavored (natural)
  yogurt
1 tablespoon lemon juice
fresh coriander leaves

Cut the eggplants into thick slices, then again into thick sticks. Put them into a large sieve and sprinkle with salt. Let stand for 30 minutes, rinse with cold water then dry on paper towels.

Heat olive oil in a large pan; fry the eggplant, stirring constantly until soft and lightly browned.

Add garlic, olives and vinegar to the pan, mix well. Transfer to a serving dish. Let stand until cold.

Mix together the tahini, yogurt and lemon juice. Drop teaspoonfuls of the mixture over the salad. Garnish with the coriander leaves.

Preparation time 15 minutes plus standing time
Cooking time 5 minutes
Serves 4

Note: The salting of the eggplants ensures that all the bitter juices are drained off. Tahini is a crushed sesame paste. It is available from large supermarkets and specialty food stores.

GOLDEN RICE RING

1 cup (5 oz, 150 g) easy cook long-grain rice
15 oz (450 g) can crushed pineapple in natural juice
1 yellow bell pepper (capsicum)
½ cup (2 oz, 50 g) toasted flaked almonds
3 tablespoons vegetable oil
1 tablespoon garlic vinegar
salt and freshly ground black pepper

Put rice into a pan. Drain juice from pineapple, make up juice to 2 cups, (¾ pint, 450 ml) with water. Add to the pan, bring to the boil, cover pan, reduce heat and simmer for about 20 minutes or until all the liquid has been absorbed. Remove from the heat, let stand until cold.

Cut 6 small diamond shapes from the yellow bell pepper, put them onto the bottom of a 5 cup (2 pint, 1¼ l) capacity ring mold.

Finely chop the remaining pepper. Add to the cooled rice with the pineapple, almonds, oil, vinegar, salt and pepper. Put this into the ring mold, pressing down well. Chill for about 1 hour. Turn out onto a plate to serve.

Preparation time 15 minutes plus standing time
Cooking time 20 minutes
Serves 4

Note: If you do not have a ring mold, serve the salad out of a glass salad bowl and arrange the pepper diamonds on top.

GREEK SALAD

1 crisp lettuce
4 large tomatoes, cut into wedges
1 cucumber, cut into large cubes
1 red bell pepper (capsicum),
    seeded and chopped
1 green bell pepper (capsicum),
    seeded and chopped
6 oz (175 g) Fetta cheese, cubed
½ cup (2 oz, 50 g) black olives
1 red onion, sliced
4 tablespoons olive oil
2 tablespoons wine vinegar
1 clove garlic, crushed
1 tablespoon chopped fresh
    marjoram or 1 teaspoon dried
    marjoram

Tear the lettuce into large pieces, put it into a salad bowl.

Add the tomatoes, cucumber and bell peppers. Arrange the Fetta cheese, olives and onion on top.

Put the dressing ingredients into a screwtop jar. Shake well then pour over salad.

Preparation time 15 minutes
Serves 4 to 5

Variation: A mild white crumbly cheese could be used instead of the Fetta cheese.

GRILLED PEPPER SALAD

2 large red bell peppers
   (capsicum)
2 large green bell peppers
   (capsicum)
2 large yellow bell peppers
   (capsicum)
3 tablespoons olive oil
1 clove garlic, crushed
salt and freshly ground black
   pepper

Cut the bell peppers into quarters, discard the seeds. Lay on a baking sheet skin side up.

Broil (grill) until the skin begins to turn brown and blister. Remove from the heat, let stand until cool enough to handle, then peel off the skin.

Cut each piece of bell pepper in half again. Arrange in a shallow dish.

Mix the olive oil with the garlic, salt and pepper. Pour over the bell peppers.

Preparation time 10 minutes plus cooling time
Cooking time 5 minutes
Serves 4 to 6

Advance preparation: These bell peppers can be prepared up to 1 day in advance. Keep covered in the refrigerator but bring to room temperature to serve.

Variation: Omit the yellow bell pepper and arrange the grilled red and green bell peppers with some sliced yellow tomatoes when available.

HOT CHICKEN SALAD

*1 cooked chicken, about 2½ lb
(1.25 kg)*
1 onion, chopped
2 tablespoons vegetable oil
*1 × 10 oz (300 g) can condensed
cream of chicken soup*
3 tablespoons mayonnaise
juice of 1 lemon
*1 green bell pepper (capsicum),
chopped*
6 sticks celery, sliced
*salt and freshly ground black
pepper*
*1 cup (4 oz, 125 g) cheddar cheese,
finely grated*
*1 cup (2 oz, 50 g) crushed potato
chips (crisps)*

Remove chicken meat from the bones and cut it into chunks. Put it into a shallow ovenproof dish.

Fry onion in oil until soft,then add to the soup with mayonnaise, lemon juice, green bell pepper and celery. Taste and adjust seasoning. Spread mixture over the chicken.

Mix together cheese and potato chips. Spinkle over the dish in an even layer.

Cook in a preheated oven 370°F (180°C, Gas Mark 5) for 35 to 40 minutes until the top is crisp and browned.

Preparation time 15 minutes
Cooking time 40 minutes
Serves 4

Advance preparation: This dish can be prepared before cooking up to 1 day in advance. Keep covered and chilled.

HOT GOAT CHEESE SALAD

4 slices French bread
2 teaspoons garlic butter
8 oz (250 g) goat cheese, sliced
    into 4
6 oz (175 g) mixed salad leaves
4 teaspoons walnut oil
½ cup (2 oz, 50 g) walnut halves

Toast the French bread on one side only. Spread the untoasted side with garlic butter, then top with a slice of goat cheese. Broil (grill) until cheese is bubbling and golden brown.

Divide the salad leaves among 4 plates. Sprinkle with the walnut oil and arrange the walnut halves on top.

Put a goat cheese toast in the middle of each plate then serve immediately.

Preparation time 10 minutes
Cooking time 5 minutes
Serves 4

INDONESIAN NOODLE AND VEGETABLE SALAD

4 oz (125 g) Chinese rice noodles
salt
2 cups (4 oz, 125 g) Nappa
    cabbage (Chinese leaves),
    shredded
2 cups (4 oz, 125 g) bean sprouts
1 × 8 oz (250 g) can bamboo
    shoots, drained
¼ cucumber, sliced
1 cup (8 oz, 250 g) carrots, thickly
    sliced
1 bunch scallions (green onions,
    spring onions), sliced
1 small onion, finely chopped
1 clove garlic, crushed
1 teaspoon grated fresh ginger
1 tablespoon peanut oil
½ cup (4 oz, 125 g) crunchy
    peanut butter
1¼ cups (½ pint, 300 ml) water
juice of ½ lemon
1 tablespoon soft brown sugar
pinch chili powder to taste

Put noodles into a pan of lightly salted boiling water. Let stand for 5 minutes. Drain, then rinse under cold water. Transfer to a shallow serving dish.

Mix together the Nappa cabbage, bean sprouts and bamboo shoots. Put on top of the noodles.

Arrange the cucumber slices around the outside edge of the salad. Arrange the carrots inside the cucumber circle. Put the scallions into the middle of the dish.

Cook the onion, garlic and ginger in a small pan until soft. Add the peanut butter, lemon juice, water, sugar and chili powder. Bring to the boil, stirring constantly. Serve this hot peanut dressing with the salad.

Preparation time 20 minutes
Cooking time 5 minutes
Serves 4

ITALIAN ANTIPASTO SALAD

1 curly endive
8 slices mortadella sausage
12 slices Italian salami
1 × 14 oz (425 g) can artichoke
*   hearts, drained*
6 oz (175 g) mozzarella cheese,
*   sliced*
4 tomatoes, quartered
3 tablespoons olive oil
1 tablespoon lemon juice
1 clove garlic, crushed
½ teaspoon dried basil
salt and freshly ground black
*   pepper*
fresh basil leaves

Line an oval platter with the endive leaves.

Roll up the mortadella then arrange it decoratively with the salami and other salad ingredients on top of the endive.

Mix together the remaining dressing ingredients, drizzle over the salad then garnish with the fresh basil leaves.

Preparation time 15 minutes
Serves 4

Variation: This is a versatile salad. To increase the portions, tuna fish, hard-cooked eggs and olives could be added.

LAMBS LETTUCE WITH PALM HEARTS AND PARMESAN CHEESE

6 oz (175 g) lambs lettuce (mâche)
15 oz (450 g) can palm hearts, drained
2 tablespoons sunflower oil
1 tablespoon hazelnut oil
1 garlic clove, crushed
1 tablespoon lemon juice
salt and freshly ground black pepper
2–3 oz (50–75 g) piece fresh Parmesan cheese

Divide the lambs lettuce among 4 plates. Slice the palm hearts and arrange on top of the lettuce.

Mix together the oils, garlic, lemon juice, salt and pepper. Pour over the salads.

Shave the Parmesan cheese into flakes with a potato peeler or mandoline slicer. Sprinkle over salads. Serve at once.

Preparation time 15 minutes
Serves 4

Watchpoint: Do not prepare the cheese until just before serving as it dries out very quickly.

Variation: Substitute artichoke hearts or canned celery hearts for the palm hearts, if desired.

LATTICED MEDITERRANEAN SALAD

*16 oz (450 g) cooked waxy
  potatoes, sliced*
*2 × 7 oz (200 g) cans tuna fish in
  oil*
2 tablespoons lemon juice
freshly ground black pepper
4 large tomatoes, sliced
4 hard-cooked eggs, sliced
*1 × 2 oz (50 g) can anchovy
  fillets, drained*
½ cup (2 oz, 50 g) black olives

Put the potatoes onto the bottom of a shallow dish.

Drain tuna, reserving 2 tablespoons oil and discarding the remainder. Flake the tuna and add to the potatoes.

Mix the tuna oil with the lemon juice and black pepper. Sprinkle over the tuna.

Arrange the tomato slices over the top of the tuna, then put a slice of egg on top of each tomato slice.

Cut the anchovies in half lengthwise, arrange in a lattice over the top of the eggs. Place the olives between the anchovy strips.

Preparation time 25 minutes
Serves 6

Note: This would make an ideal dish for a buffet party. For a special occasion use fresh cooked tuna fish instead of canned.

LAYERED CHEESE AND HAM SALAD

3 tablespoons mayonnaise
1 tablespoon sunflower oil
1 tablespoon white wine vinegar
salt and freshly ground black
  pepper
1 small iceberg lettuce, shredded
1½ cups (6 oz, 175 g) cheddar
  cheese, grated
4 sticks celery, sliced
6 oz (175 g) smoked ham, diced
1 small red bell pepper
  (capsicum), sliced into rings
1 bunch mustard and cress, or
  parsley

Mix together the dressing ingredients.

Put half the lettuce into the bottom of a deep glass salad bowl.

Add half the dressing, then layer up the cheese, celery, ham and other half of the lettuce. Top with the remaining dressing.

Arrange the red bell pepper around the edge of the bowl, then fill the center with the mustard and cress.

Preparation time 20 minutes
Serves 4

Variation: Use chicken or turkey instead of the ham. The type of cheese used could also be varied.

LIME AND CORIANDER FISH SALAD

1¼ lb (625 g) monkfish (or
  snapper)
grated rind and juice of 1 large
  juicy lime
1 small green hot chili pepper,
  seeds removed and finely
  chopped
½ small green bell pepper
  (capsicum), finely chopped
2 tablespoons fresh coriander,
  chopped
1 scallion (spring onion, shallot),
  finely chopped
1 tablespoon olive oil
½ teaspoon ground cumin
salt
1 crisp lettuce
1 avocado, peeled and sliced

Cut the monkfish into slices, discarding any bones.

Put the fish into a pan, cover with cold water, bring to simmering point, remove from the heat, cover pan and let stand for 10 minutes. Drain fish, put into a glass or ceramic dish.

Mix together the lime rind and juice, peppers, coriander, scallion, oil, cumin and salt. Pour over fish. Let stand until fish is quite cold, turning the fish from time to time.

Put the lettuce and avocado on a serving dish and arrange the fish and dressing on top.

Preparation time 15 minutes
Cooking time 5 minutes
Serves 4

MEXICAN TACO SALAD

1 small crisp lettuce, shredded
2 large tomatoes, diced
1 avocado, peeled and stoned
1 tablespoon lime juice
2 tablespoons sunflower oil
pinch chili powder, or to taste
8 oz (250 g) chorizo sausage, sliced
8 taco shells
1 cup (4 oz, 125 g) Monterey Jack
  or cheddar cheese, grated
¾ cup (¼ pint, 150 ml) sour
  cream
8 leaves fresh coriander

Put lettuce, tomatoes and avocado into a bowl.

Mix together lime juice, oil and chili powder; add to the bowl and mix well.

Divide chorizo sausage among the taco shells, then add the salad and the cheese.

Top each taco with a teaspoon of sour cream, garnish each one with a fresh coriander leaf.

Preparation time 20 minutes
Serves 4

Variation: This salad could also be layered up onto a Tostado (a fried corn pancake) available in packets from large supermarkets.

MIDDLE EASTERN PILAF SALAD

⅓ cup (2 oz, 50 g) wild rice
2½ cups (1 pint, 600 ml) boiling
  water
salt
¾ cup (4 oz, 125 g) easy cook
  long-grain white rice
¾ cup (4 oz, 125 g) ready to eat
  dried apricots, halved
¾ cup (4 oz, 125 g) ready to eat
  dried figs, halved
1 teaspoon powdered cinnamon
1 teaspoon powdered allspice
2 tablespoons peanut oil
1 tablespoon lemon juice
freshly ground black pepper
¼ cup (1 oz, 25 g) pine nuts or
  almonds, toasted

Cook wild rice in boiling salted water in a covered pan for 20 minutes.

Add white rice to the pan, stir gently to mix, then cook for a further 20 minutes. Drain if necessary then transfer to a bowl.

Add apricots and figs to the bowl.

Mix together cinnamon, allspice, oil, lemon juice and pepper. Stir into rice.

Let stand until cold, then sprinkle with the pine nuts.

Preparation time 15 minutes plus standing time
Cooking time 40 minutes
Serves 4 to 6

Advance preparation: This salad can be prepared up to 1 day in advance. Do not add the nuts until just before serving.

MIXED BEAN SALAD

1 cup (6 oz, 175 g) canned
   garbanzos (chick peas)
1 cup (6 oz, 175 g) canned black
   eyed beans
1 cup (6 oz, 175 g) canned
   flageolet beans
½ cup (4 oz, 125 g) carrots, cut
   into thin strips
1 small red bell pepper (capsicum)
   cut into thin strips
1 small onion, finely chopped
1 clove garlic, crushed
1 tablespoon cider vinegar
2 tablespoons vegetable oil
½ teaspoon dried tarragon
salt and freshly ground black
   pepper

Mix the garbanzos, beans, carrots and bell pepper together in a large bowl.

Mix the onion and garlic with the vinegar, oil, tarragon, salt and pepper. Pour onto the beans and vegetables and mix thoroughly.

Preparation time 15 minutes
Serves 4 to 6

Note: Any other canned beans could be used, as long as the total weight is kept. Alternatively, try substituting one of the canned beans with an equal amount of lightly cooked fresh green beans.

NUTTY WHOLEWHEAT SALAD

*2 cups (8 oz, 250 g) cooked
    wholewheat grain*
*¾ cup (3 oz, 75 g) salted cashew
    nuts*
2 tablespoons peanut oil
*2 cups (16 oz, 500 g) cottage
    cheese*
*½ small cucumber, cut into small
    cubes*
*bunch scallions (spring onions),
    sliced*
*salt and freshly ground black
    pepper*
1 tablespoon chopped fresh chives

Mix together wholewheat grain, cashew nuts and oil Arrange in a ring on a round serving platter.

Combine the cottage cheese, cucumber and scallions, season to taste. Fill the center of the wholewheat ring with the cottage cheese mixture.

Serve sprinkled with the chopped chives.

Preparation time 15 minutes
Serves 4

Advance preparation: Wholewheat grain needs to be prepared in advance. Soak 1 cup (4 oz, 125 g) grain in cold water for 2 to 3 hours. Cook in boiling water for about 30 minutes until tender. Drain well then let stand until cold.

PEAR AND WATERCRESS SALAD

1 bunch watercress
4 ripe pears, peeled and cored
3 oz (75 g) creamy blue cheese
2 tablespoons unflavored (natural)
*   Greek yogurt*
1 tablespoon vegetable oil
freshly ground black pepper
1 bunch scallions (spring onions),
*   chopped*

Line a round serving plate with the watercress. Slice the pears and arrange in overlapping slices over the watercress.

Crumble the blue cheese into the yogurt, add the oil and pepper. Beat well then pour over the pears. Sprinkle with the scallions and serve immediately.

Preparation time 15 minutes
Serves 4

Advance preparation: This salad can be prepared 2 to 3 hours in advance, but brush the pear slices with lemon juice to prevent them from going brown.

Note: Suitable cheeses for this salad are Dolcelatte, Bleu de Bresse or Pipo Creme.

PIQUANT HERRING SALAD

8 to 12 rollmop herrings,
  depending on size
4 sweet and sour pickled
  cucumbers, cut into cubes
2 teaspoons capers
⅔ cup (¼ pint, 150 ml) sour
  cream or yogurt
2 tablespoons chopped fresh dill
lettuce leaves
1 onion, sliced

Cut the herrings into strips. Put them into a bowl, then add the pickled cucumbers, capers, sour cream and dill.

Line a serving dish with lettuce leaves, put the herring salad on top then garnish with the onion rings.

Preparation time 15 minutes
Serves 4

RED AND WHITE CABBAGE SALAD

2 cups (8 oz, 250 g) red cabbage,
  shredded
2 cups (8 oz, 250 g) Dutch white
  cabbage, shredded
2 large firm bananas
1 tablespoon lemon juice
1 cup (2 oz, 50 g) toasted flaked
  (desiccated) coconut
3 tablespoons mayonnaise
salt and freshly ground black
  pepper

Put the shredded cabbage into a salad bowl.

Thinly slice the bananas, brush with lemon juice, and add to the bowl with the coconut.

Stir in the mayonnaise, salt and pepper and mix well.

Preparation time 15 minutes
Serves 4 to 6

Variation: If only over-ripe bananas are available, mash them with the lemon juice and add them to the salad with the mayonnaise.

SALAD KEBABS

1 large red bell pepper (capsicum)
1 large green bell pepper
(capsicum)
½ cucumber
8 oz (250 g) piece Edam or Gouda
cheese
16 radishes
16 cherry tomatoes
shredded lettuce
2–3 tablespoons vinaigrette
dressing

Cut the red and green bell peppers, cucumber and cheese each into 16 pieces.

Thread the cheese and vegetables onto 8 wooden kebab skewers, alternating the colors and textures, starting and ending with a cherry tomato.

Put the shredded lettuce onto an oval serving dish. Arrange the kebabs on top.

Serve sprinkled with the vinaigrette dressing.

Preparation time 15 minutes
Serves 4

Variation: Any other suitable vegetables can be used in this recipe. Try chunks of carrot or cauliflower florets and experiment with different types of cheese.

SALAD-STUFFED OMELET ROLL

2 teaspoons vegetable oil
6 eggs
½ cup (2 oz, 50 g) cheddar cheese,
    finely grated
salt and freshly ground black
    pepper
½ small crisp lettuce, shredded
½ cup (4 oz, 125 g) carrots, grated
1 small orange bell pepper
    (capsicum), thinly sliced
1 small avocado, cut into cubes
1 tablespoon lemon juice
2 tablespoons mayonnaise

Line a 12 inch × 9 inch (30 × 23 cm) jelly roll (Swiss roll) pan with wax (greaseproof) paper. Brush the paper with oil.

Beat the eggs, add the cheese, salt and pepper. Pour into pan.

Cook in a preheated oven 375°F (190°C, Gas Mark 5) for 5 minutes until just set.

Remove from the oven, turn out onto another sheet of wax (greaseproof) paper. Peel off the lining paper and let stand until cold.

Mix together the lettuce, carrots and bell pepper. Toss the avocado in the lemon juice; add to the other ingredients. Gently combine all ingredients with the mayonnaise.

Arrange the salad in an even layer over the omelet. Roll up like a jelly roll (Swiss roll). Wrap tightly in the paper twisting the ends to secure. Chill for at least 30 minutes.

Trim the edges and cut into thick slices to serve.

Preparation time 20 minutes plus chilling time
Cooking time 5 minutes
Serves 4 to 6

Note: Do not overcook the omelet otherwise it will become tough and rubbery.

SALADE PAYSANNE

4 oz (125 g) fine green (French)
    beans
salt
1 lb (500 g) small new potatoes,
    cooked in their skins and cooled
4 tomatoes, cut into wedges
2 pickled cucumbers, chopped
1 small onion, finely chopped
1 clove garlic, crushed
3 tablespoons mayonnaise
1 tablespoon white wine vinegar
freshly ground black pepper
12 hard-cooked quails eggs or 3
    hard-cooked hens eggs,
    quartered
1 tablespoon chopped fresh parsley

Cook the beans in lightly salted water for 5 minutes. Drain and cool. Put them into a salad bowl with the potatoes, tomatoes and pickled cucumbers.

Combine the onion, garlic, mayonnaise, vinegar and black pepper; add to the bowl and mix well.

Arrange the quails eggs on top of the salad, then sprinkle with the chopped parsley.

Preparation time 20 minutes
Cooking time 5 minutes
Serves 4 to 6

SALADE ROUGE

1 × 1 lb (500 g) can red kidney
    beans, drained
6 oz (175 g) cooked beets
    (beetroot) peeled and cubed
6 oz (175 g) red cabbage, shredded
3 tablespoons vegetable oil
1 tablespoon tarragon vinegar
1 teaspoon ground cumin
salt and freshly ground black
    pepper
1 small radiccio or other red
    leaved lettuce
1 small red onion, sliced

Combine the beans, beets and red cabbage in a bowl. Add the oil, vinegar, cumin, salt and pepper. Mix well.

Line a shallow glass bowl with the radiccio leaves. Pile the red salad into the center. Top with the red onion slices.

Preparation time 15 minutes
Serves 5 to 6

Advance preparation: This salad is especially good if prepared in advance to allow the flavors to develop. Do not prepare the lettuce until just before serving.

SALAMI, HAM AND FENNEL SALAD

3 oz (75 g) Milano salami, sliced
8 oz (250 g) cooked ham, diced
8 oz (250 g) Daikon radish
  (mooli) thinly sliced
1 large head Florence fennel
3 tablespoons olive oil
1 tablespoon red wine vinegar
1 clove garlic, crushed
½ teaspoon dried oregano
freshly ground black pepper
1 small lettuce
½ cup (2 oz, 50 g) pimento stuffed
  olives, sliced

Cut salami into strips; put into a bowl with the ham and radish.

Thinly slice the fennel, reserving any leaves, then add to the bowl.

Mix together the oil, vinegar, garlic, oregano and pepper. Pour into the bowl and mix well.

Line a serving dish with the lettuce leaves. Transfer the salad to the serving dish. Sprinkle with the olives and garnish with the fennel leaves.

Preparation time 20 minutes
Serves 4 to 6

Variation: Any other type of salami could be used and celery could replace the fennel if desired.

SCALLOP SALAD

1 lb (500 g) scallops with corals
2 cups (8 oz, 250 g) button
   mushrooms
1 cup (4 oz, 125 g) canned water
   chestnuts
1 tablespoon lemon juice
1 tablespoon dry vermouth
4 tablespoons olive oil
½ teaspoon ground turmeric
salt and freshly ground black
   pepper
1 teaspoon ground paprika

Separate the white part of the scallops from the corals.
Lightly poach the white part in boiling water for 3
minutes; add the corals and poach for a further 2
minutes. Drain the scallops, put the whites and corals
into separate bowls, let stand until cold.

Add the mushrooms and water chestnuts to the white
scallops. Add the lemon juice, vermouth, oil, turmeric,
salt and pepper. Mix well.

Divide mixture among 4 scallop shells or small dishes.

Garnish with scallop corals then sprinkle with paprika.

Preparation time 20 minutes
Cooking time 5 minutes
Serves 4

Note: This salad makes an ideal first course or a light
lunch or supper dish if served with a green salad.

SMOKED SALMON AND AVOCADO SALAD

4 oz (125 g) smoked salmon, cut into strips
4 sticks celery, sliced
1 bunch scallions (spring onions), sliced
4 ripe avocados
2 tablespoons lemon juice
2 tablespoons mayonnaise
2 tablespoons sour cream
1 teaspoon tomato ketchup
few drops Tabasco sauce
salt and freshly ground black pepper
¼ cup (1 oz, 25 g) toasted flaked almonds

Put smoked salmon into a bowl with the celery and scallions.

Cut avocados in half, discard stones. Remove flesh from avocado with a teaspoon. Reserve the avocado skins.

Add the avocado flesh to the bowl with the lemon juice. Mix gently with the salmon and celery then spoon the mixture back into the avocado skins.

Mix together mayonnaise, sour cream, ketchup and Tabasco, taste and adjust seasoning. Spread over the top of the avocados. Sprinkle with the flaked almonds and serve immediately.

Preparation time 15 minutes
Serves 4

SPICED LENTIL SALAD

1 cup (6 oz, 175 g) small brown
   French lentils
1 small onion, chopped
1 teaspoon grated fresh ginger
3 tablespoons peanut oil
½ teaspoon ground turmeric
½ teaspoon ground cumin
1 teaspoon garam masala
cayenne pepper, to taste
1 tablespoon wine vinegar
1 tablespoon lemon juice
fresh coriander leaves

Cook lentils in boiling water for about 35 to 40 minutes until just tender, then drain well.

Fry onion and ginger in oil until soft. Add the turmeric, cumin, garam masala and pepper, cook for 1 minute.

Add lentils to the pan, stir around until coated with the spices. Remove from the heat, stir in the vinegar and lemon juice.

Transfer to a serving dish. Let stand until cold then garnish with the coriander leaves.

Preparation time 15 minutes plus cooling time
Cooking time 35 to 40 minutes
Serves 4

Note: Small French lentils, sometimes known as lentils de Puy, are available from health food stores and specialty food stores. Red lentils could be used instead but these tend to break up when cooking.

SPRING VEGETABLE SALAD

¾ cup (4 oz, 125 g) shelled fava
    beans (broad beans)
¾ cup (4 oz, 125 g) shelled peas
8 oz (250 g) cherry tomatoes
1 small cauliflower, cut into
    florets
4 tablespoons pesto
2 tablespoons olive oil
1 tablespoon lemon juice
fresh basil leaves

Cook the beans and peas in boiling water for 5 minutes. Drain and rinse under cold running water to cool. Put into a salad bowl; add the tomatoes and cauliflower.

Mix together the pesto, oil and lemon juice. Pour into the bowl, mix gently but thoroughly. Garnish with the fresh basil leaves.

Preparation time 15 minutes
Cooking time 5 minutes
Serves 4

Note: Pesto is an Italian basil sauce available in jars from large supermarkets, specialty food stores and delicatessens. When fresh beans and peas are out of season the equivalent amount of frozen vegetables can be used.

SPROUTED BEAN SALAD
WITH EXOTIC FRUIT

*4 cups (8 oz, 250 g) alfalfa or
other sprouted beans*
*12 lychees, peeled and seeds
removed*
4 oz (125 g) tofu
2 tablespoons sunflower oil
1 tablespoon lemon juice
2 passion fruit
*salt and freshly ground black
pepper*
1 small pineapple, peeled
1 papaya (paw paw) peeled

Put the alfalfa sprouts around the edge of a serving dish; arrange the lychees on top.

Mash the tofu with the oil and lemon juice to make a smooth paste.

Cut the passion fruit in half, scoop out the seeds and juice and add to the tofu. Taste and adjust seasoning.

Cut the pineapple into cubes, discarding the woody core. Discard the seeds from the papaya and cut into cubes. Add the pineapple and papaya to the tofu dressing. Mix gently then put into the center of the alfalfa sprouts.

Preparation time 15 minutes
Serves 4

Note: When buying passion fruit look for skins that are shrivelled as this indicates a ripe fruit.

STEAK SALAD

1½ lb (750 g) sirloin (rump) steak,
  in one thick piece, or the
  remains of a cooked beef roast
1 romaine (cos) lettuce
1 bunch scallions (spring onions),
  cut into strips
4 tablespoons olive oil
2 tablespoons red wine vinegar
½ teaspoon black peppercorns,
  roughly crushed
1 teaspoon chopped fresh tarragon
1 tablespoon chopped fresh mint
1 tablespoon chopped fresh parsley
1 teaspoon Dijon-style mustard
salt

Remove any fat from the steak. Broil (grill) for 3 to 6 minutes each side, depending on how you like your steak cooked.

Arrange the lettuce leaves at each end of an oval serving platter. Sprinkle the scallions over the top.

Beat the olive oil and vinegar together in a large bowl. Add the peppercorns, herbs, mustard and salt.

When the steak is cooked, cut into thin strips, add to the herb dressing then let stand until cold. Transfer to the middle of the platter.

Preparation time 15 minutes plus standing time
Cooking time 6 to 12 minutes
Serves 4

STEAMED VEGETABLE SALAD

1 cup (8 oz, 250 g) baby carrots,
   peeled
4 oz (125 g) thin asparagus
8 oz (250 g) baby zucchini
   (courgettes), with ends removed
¾ cup (4 oz, 125 g) shelled young
   fava (broad) beans
3 tablespoons olive oil
1 tablespoon red wine vinegar
1 teaspoon sugar
1 teaspoon tomato paste (purée)
2 ripe tomatoes, skinned and
   seeded
1 teaspoon chopped fresh basil or
   ½ teaspoon dried basil
salt and freshly ground black
   pepper

Layer up the carrots, asparagus, zucchini and beans in a steamer, if possible a bamboo Chinese steamer. Cover the steamer and place over a pan of boiling water. Steam for about 10 to 15 minutes. The vegetables should remain quite crisp.

Beat together the oil, vinegar, sugar and tomato paste.

Cut the tomatoes into very small pieces, add to the oil with the basil, salt and pepper.

Arrange the vegetables decoratively on a serving dish. Pour the dressing over the vegetables.

Preparation time 15 minutes
Cooking time 10 to 15 minutes
Serves 4

Variation: Other small vegetables such as baby sweetcorn or baby leeks could be used.

Note: This salad is best if served lukewarm or at room temperature.

SWEET AND SOUR MUSHROOM SALAD

*2 cups (8 oz, 250 g) button
    mushrooms*
*2 cups (8 oz, 250 g) oyster
    mushrooms*
*2 cups (8 oz, 250 g) shii-take
    mushrooms*
1 small onion, chopped
1 tablespoon sunflower oil
1 tablespoon tomato ketchup
*½ cup (4 fl oz, 125 ml) pineapple
    juice*
1 tablespoon white wine vinegar
1 tablespoon soft brown sugar
*salt and freshly ground black
    pepper*

Trim the stalks from the mushrooms and wash if necessary.

Fry onion in oil in a large pan, until soft. Add ketchup, pineapple juice, vinegar, sugar, salt and pepper; bring to the boil, reduce heat, simmer for 2 to 3 minutes to reduce liquid to half.

Add mushrooms to the pan. Stir around until coated with the liquid. Transfer mushrooms to a serving dish. Let stand until cold.

Preparation time 15 minutes plus standing time
Cooking time 5 minutes
Serves 4 to 6

Variation: If oyster and shii-take mushrooms are unavailable, use all button mushrooms.

SWEET POTATO
AND ANCHOVY SALAD

1½ lb (750 g) sweet potatoes
salt
1 small onion, finely chopped
1 × 2 oz (50 g) can anchovy
   fillets, drained and chopped
1 tablespoon boiling water
1 tablespoon white wine vinegar
2 tablespoons mayonnaise
freshly ground black pepper
1 × 4 oz (125 g) head Belgian
   endive (chicory)
1 tablespoon chopped fresh dill

Scrub the sweet potatoes, cut into large even-sized pieces, cook in boiling salted water for 15 to 20 minutes until just tender. Drain, let stand until cool enough to handle, then peel and cut into cubes.

Put onion and anchovies into a bowl, add boiling water and vinegar, then add sweet potatoes, mayonnaise and black pepper. Mix gently.

Cut endive in half lengthwise, separate the leaves then arrange them around the inside edge of a salad bowl. Put the potato salad into the bowl. Serve sprinkled with the chopped dill.

Preparation time 15 minutes
Cooking time 20 minutes
Serves 4

Watchpoint: Keep testing the potatoes while cooking as they will disintegrate if overcooked.

TRICOLOR SALAD

1 lb (500 g) broccoli florets
salt
4 oz (125 g) sun-dried tomatoes in
  oil
½ teaspoon dried thyme
1 tablespoon lemon juice
freshly ground black pepper
4 oz (125 g) mozzarella cheese, cut
  into cubes

Cook the broccoli in boiling salted water for 3 minutes. Drain well then transfer to a serving dish.

Cut the sun-dried tomatoes in half if large; add to the broccoli with 2 tablespoons of oil from jar, the thyme, lemon juice and black pepper. Let stand until cold, then gently stir in the mozzarella cheese.

Preparation time 15 minutes plus standing time
Cooking time 3 minutes
Serves 4

Note: Sun-dried tomatoes are available in jars from larger supermarkets and specialty food stores. If they are unavailable use 8 oz (250 g) fresh tomatoes and 2 tablespoons olive oil.

Tuna and Pasta Salad

8 oz (250 g) dried pasta shells
salt
1 × 7 oz (200 g) can tuna fish in oil
bunch scallions (spring onions), sliced
1 red bell pepper (capsicum), sliced
¾ cup (4 oz, 125 g) sweetcorn kernels
juice of 1 lemon
3–4 tablespoons mayonnaise
freshly ground black pepper

Cook pasta in salted boiling water for 8 to 10 minutes until just cooked. Drain well then transfer to a large bowl.

Pour the oil from the tuna onto the pasta, mix well then let stand until cold.

Add the remaining ingredients to the bowl, mixing well.

Preparation time 15 minutes
Cooking time 10 minutes
Serves 4

Advance preparation: Preparing this salad up to 1 day in advance allows the flavors to develop.

Variation: Any other pasta shapes could be used, or use left-over spaghetti or macaroni for a quickly prepared meal.

TUSCAN BREAD SALAD

4 large slices bread (preferably
    Italian country bread)
2 cloves garlic, crushed
4 tablespoons olive oil
1 lb (500 g) ripe tomatoes
2 tablespoons fresh basil, roughly
    chopped
salt and freshly ground black
    pepper

Rub the bread slices on both sides with the crushed garlic, then brush both sides of the bread with a little of the olive oil.

Put bread onto a baking sheet. Cook in a preheated oven 425°F (220°C, Gas Mark 7) for about 15 minutes until bread is brown and crisp.

While bread is cooking cut the tomatoes into pieces, mix with the remaining olive oil, basil, salt and pepper.

Remove bread from the oven, put each slice onto an individual plate. Put tomatoes on the bread and serve immediately.

Preparation time 10 minutes
Cooking time 15 minutes
Serves 4

WARM CAMEMBERT SALAD

8 oz (250 g) young Swiss chard (spinach) leaves
2 cups (8 oz, 250 g) small zucchini (courgettes), sliced
½ small cauliflower, cut into florets
1 green skinned apple, cored and sliced
1 tablespoon lemon juice
3 tablespoons mayonnaise
3 tablespoons sour cream
4 oz (125 g) camembert cheese, cut into small cubes
freshly ground black pepper

Put the Swiss chard, zucchini and cauliflower into a salad bowl.

Toss the apple slices in the lemon juice and add to the bowl.

Put the mayonnaise, sour cream and camembert into a small pan, heat gently, stirring constantly until hot but not boiling. Pour into the salad bowl, toss well, and serve immediately.

Preparation time 15 minutes
Cooking time 2 to 3 minutes
Serves 4

Variation: This salad could also be made with a soft creamy blue cheese.

WARM CHICKEN LIVER SALAD

1 red leaved lettuce
1 lb (500 g) chicken livers
2 tablespoons grapeseed oil
1½ cups (6 oz, 175 g) seedless
  white grapes
1 tablespoon balsamic or sherry
  vinegar
salt and freshly ground black
  pepper
¼ cup (1 oz, 25 g) pine nuts

Line 4 plates with lettuce leaves.

Trim chicken livers, rinse under cold water then dry well with paper towels.

Heat oil in a pan, add chicken livers and stir briskly until lightly browned.

Add grapes and vinegar to the pan, season to taste. Mix well then divide among plates.

Sprinkle with pine nuts and serve immediately.

Preparation time 15 minutes
Cooking time 5 minutes
Serves 4

Watchpoint: Do not overcook the chicken livers or they will become tough.

Note: Balsamic and sherry vinegars are available from large supermarkets and specialty food stores. They give a wonderful aromatic flavor to dishes.

WATERMELON AND TOMATO SALAD

4 beefsteak tomatoes, thinly sliced
½ watermelon, peeled
1 red onion, finely chopped
1 tablespoon chopped fresh mint
1 tablespoon lemon juice
1 teaspoon sugar
3 tablespoons vegetable oil
salt and freshly ground black
    pepper
fresh mint sprigs, to garnish

Line a salad bowl with the tomato slices.

Cut the watermelon into small, even-sized pieces, discarding the seeds. Arrange over the tomatoes, sprinkle with the onion.

Combine the chopped mint, lemon juice, sugar, oil, salt and pepper. Pour over the salad, then garnish with the mint sprigs.

Preparation time 15 minutes
Serves 4 to 6

Variation: When watermelons are out of season this refreshing salad can be made with a honeydew melon, but omit the sugar in the dressing.

WINTER VEGETABLE SALAD

8 oz (250 g) parsnips
8 oz (250 g) celery root (celeriac)
6 oz (175 g) kohlrabi or turnips
½ cup (3 oz, 75 g) pitted dates,
   finely chopped
½ cup (4 oz, 125 g) low fat soft
   cheese
1 tablespoon lemon juice
2 tablespoons sunflower oil
salt and freshly ground black
   pepper
12 radishes, thinly sliced

Remove the woody cores from the parsnips, then coarsely grate into a bowl.

Coarsely grate the celery root and kohlrabi and add to the bowl.

Mix the dates with the cheese, lemon juice, oil, salt and pepper. Add to the grated vegetables and mix well.

Turn the salad out into a mound on a serving plate. Scatter the radishes over the top.

Preparation time 15 minutes
Serves 4 to 6

VINAIGRETTE DRESSING

6 tablespoons sunflower or olive
    oil
2 tablespoons white wine vinegar
1 teaspoon superfine (caster) sugar
salt and freshly ground black
    pepper

Put all the ingredients into a screw-top jar and shake
vigorously. Keep refrigerated and use as required.

This is the basic vinaigrette recipe but it can be varied
by using different types of oil or vinegar or adding
garlic, mustard or herbs.

MAYONNAISE

1 egg yolk
1 teaspoon white wine vinegar
salt and white pepper
⅔ cup (¼ pint, 150 ml sunflower
    oil)

Put egg yolk into a bowl, add vinegar, salt and pepper.

Beat until mixed, then add the oil starting with a drip
at a time beating constantly until the mayonnaise
becomes thick. As the mayonnaise thickens, the oil can
be added in a steady stream.

Taste and adjust seasoning. Keep covered and
refrigerated and use within two days.

INDEX

oak leaf
    beet and orange salad 12
romaine (cos)
    steak salad 88
lime and coriander fish salad 52
liver, chicken, salad 104

màche
    lambs lettuce with palm hearts and parmesan cheese 46
mango-tout
    Chinese salad 20
mango, chicken and melon salad 18
mayonnaise 110
Mediterranean salad 48
melon, mango and chicken salad 18
mortadella sausage
    Italian antipasto salad 44
mozzarella cheese
    Italian antipasto salad 44
    tricolor salad 96
mushrooms
    scallop salad 78
    sweet and sour mushroom salad 92

Nappa cabbage
    Chinese salad 20
    Indonesian noodle and vegetable salad 42
niçoise salad, beef 10
noodle and vegetable salad, Indonesian 42
nut, raisin ad carrot salad 16

omelet roll, salad-stuffed 70
orange and beet salad 12
palm hearts with lambs lettuce and parmesan cheese 46
parsley
    cracked wheat salad 24
pasta and tuna salad 98
pear and watercress salad 62
pepper salad, grilled 36
pilaf salad, Middle Eastern 56
pineapple
    golden rice ring 32
potatoes
    salade paysanne 72
prawns
    Chinese salad 20

prosciutto
    crunchy leek salad 28

quails eggs
    salade paysanne 72

raisin, carrot and nut salad 16
rice, wild
    Middle Eastern pilaf salad 56
rice ring, golden 32

salami
    Italian antipasto salad 44
    salami, ham and fennel salad 76
salmon, smoked, and avocado salad 80
scallop salad 78
shrimp
    Chinese salad 20
snow peas
    Chinese salad 20
spring vegetable salad 84
steak salad 88
sweet and sour mushroom salad 92
sweet potato and anchovy salad 94

taco salad, Mexican 54
tahini and eggplant salad 30
tomatoes
    Tuscan bread salad 100
    watermelon and tomato salad 106
tomatoes, sun-dried
    tricolor salad 96
tuna
    and pasta salad 98
    Mediterranean salad 48

vegetable salad
    spring 84
    steamed 90
    winter 108
vinaigrette dressing 110

water chestnuts, scallop salad 78
watercress and pear salad 62
watermelon and tomato salad 106
wholewheat salad, nutty 60
winter vegetable salad 108